Carolyn Miller's

PREFACE

The purpose of this series is to increase the student's technical ability. Each book contains material designed to strengthen fingers, increase flexibility, and help the student master the many technical skills needed to perform well. *Sportacular Warmups* combines sports and music. Students can relate the musical exercise to a similar activity in the five sport areas. As a review, each section ends with a solo that incorporates various exercises from that section.

I hope students will enjoy *Sportacular Warmups* and will become "sportacular" pianists!

Carolyn Miller

CONTENTS

I. Basketball 2

II. Baseball 7

III. Track and Field..13

IV. Extreme Adventure Sports.................................18

V. Soccer 25

ISBN 978-0-87718-056-2

EXCLUSIVELY DISTRIBUTED BY

WILLIS MUSIC

HAL•LEONARD®

Visit Hal Leonard Online at
www.halleonard.com

Contact us:
Hal Leonard
7777 West Bluemound Road
Milwaukee, WI 53213
Email: info@halleonard.com

In Europe, contact:
Hal Leonard Europe Limited
42 Wigmore Street
Marylebone, London, W1U 2RN
Email: info@halleonardeurope.com

In Australia, contact:
Hal Leonard Australia Pty. Ltd.
4 Lentara Court
Cheltenham, Victoria, 3192 Australia
Email: info@halleonard.com.au

I.
BASKETBALL

1. Traveling

Can you play both hands at the same time?

2. Three Pointer

3. Jump Shot

4. Tip In
('Round the Rim and In)

Tip in!

'Round the rim and in!

Try to shoot with the left hand, starting two octaves lower.

5. Foul

6. World Championship

II.
BASEBALL
1. Seventh Inning Stretch

2. Single

3. Double

4. Triple

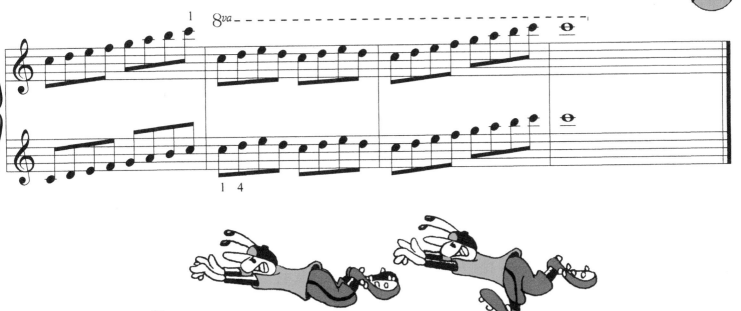

5. Double Steal

6. The Wave

7. The World Series

"Take Me Out to the Ballgame"

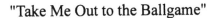

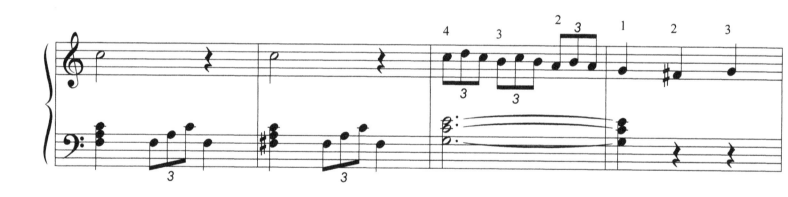

III.
TRACK AND FIELD

1. Hurdles

2. Fifty Yard Dash

5. One Hundred Yard Dash

6. Olympics

IV.
Extreme Adventure Sports

1. Free Fall

2. Rollerblading

3. Eddies

4. Wheelie

5. Rappelling

6. Sailing

7. Advanced Rappelling

8. Take It to the Limit

V.
SOCCER

1. Block

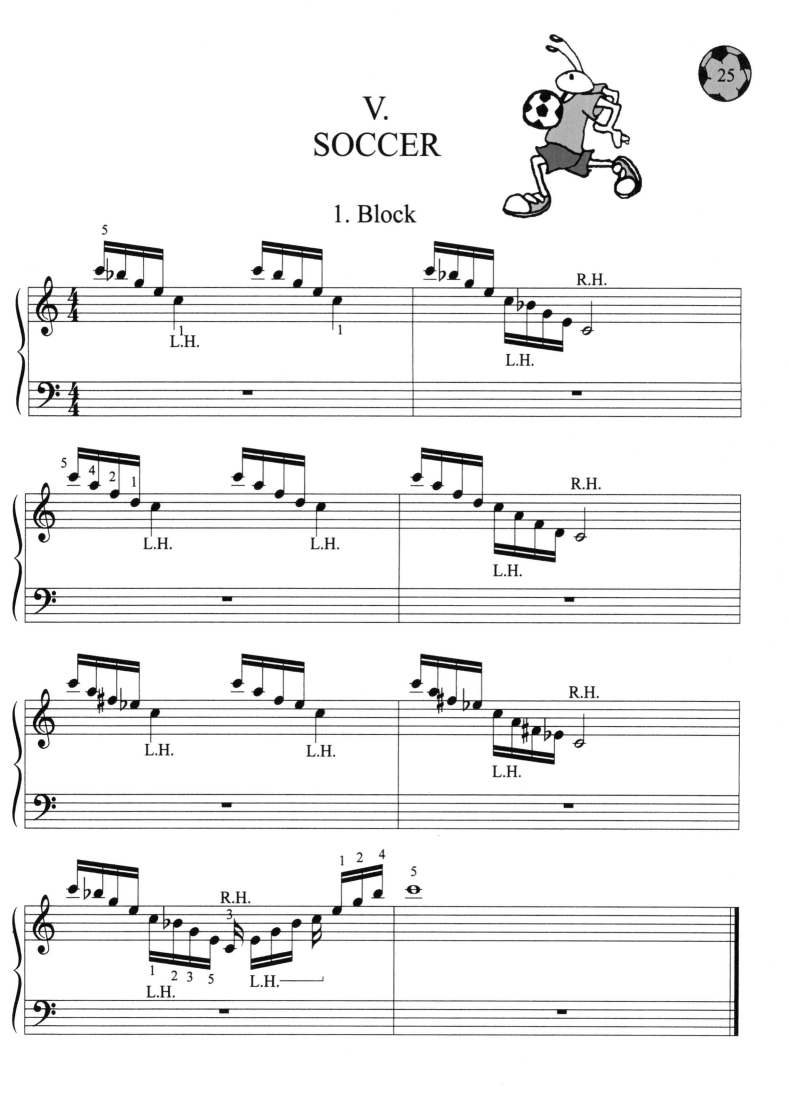

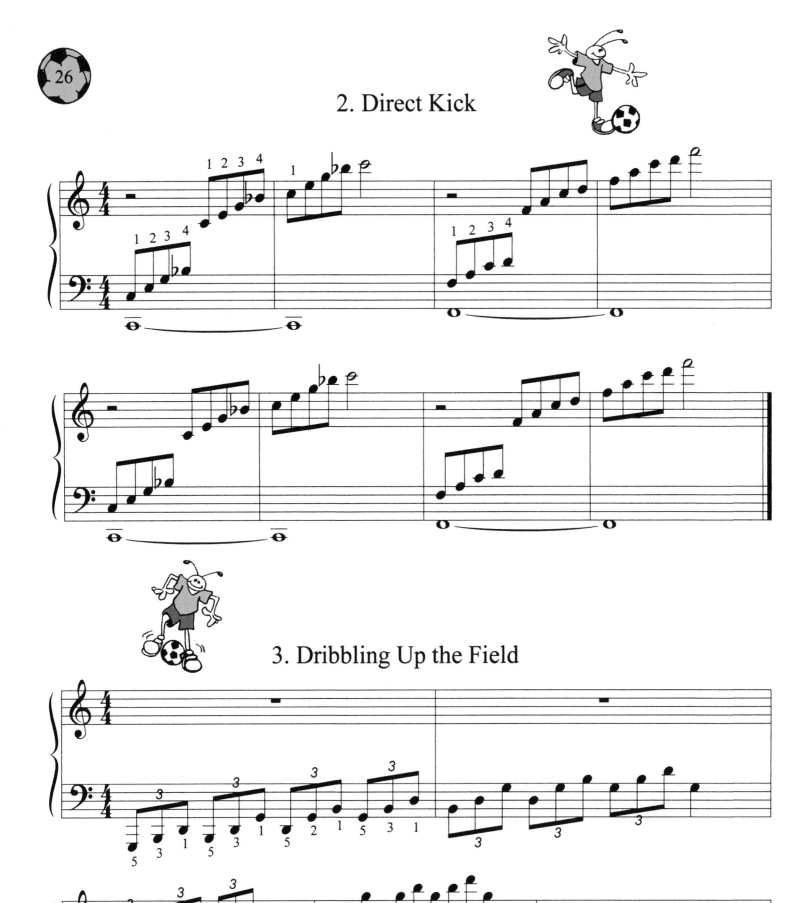

2. Direct Kick

3. Dribbling Up the Field

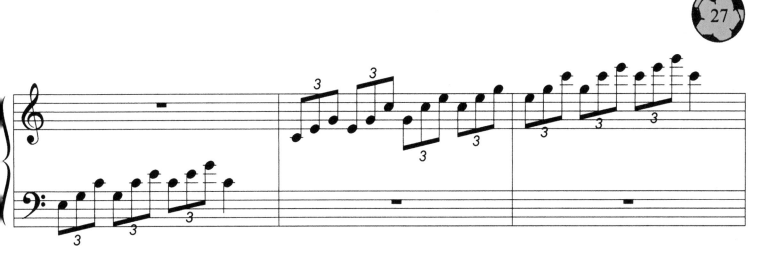
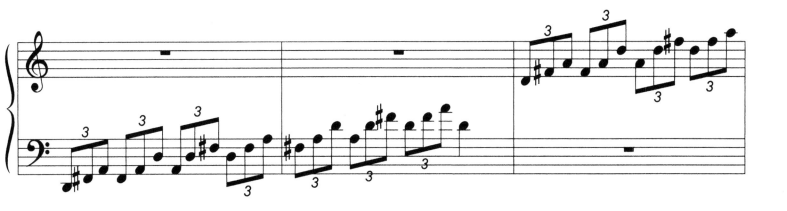
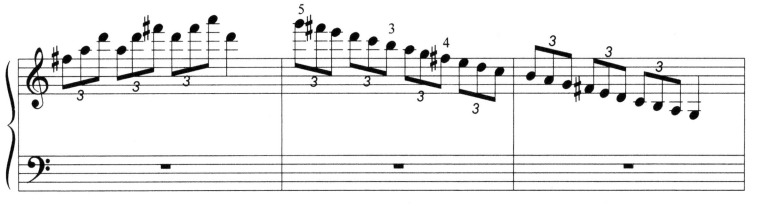
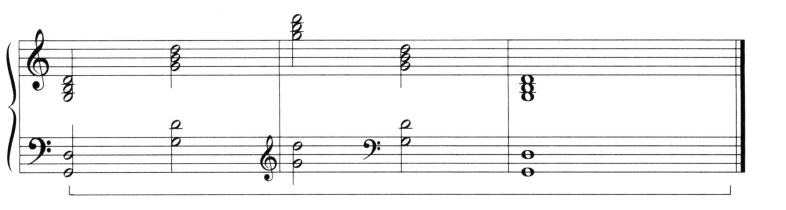

4. Juggling

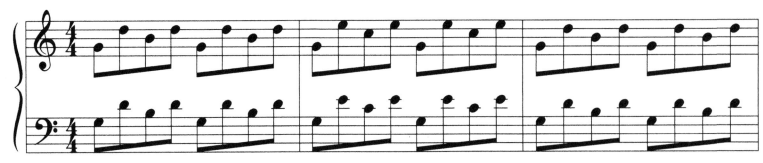

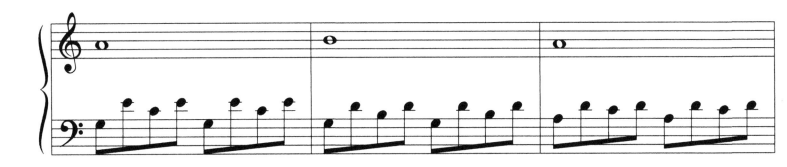

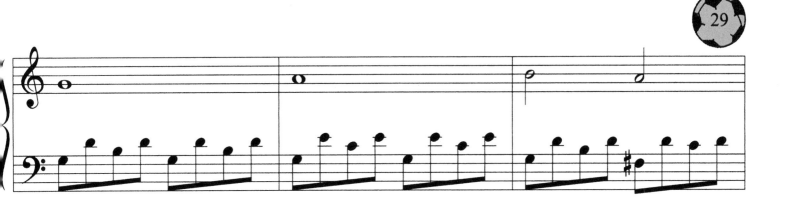

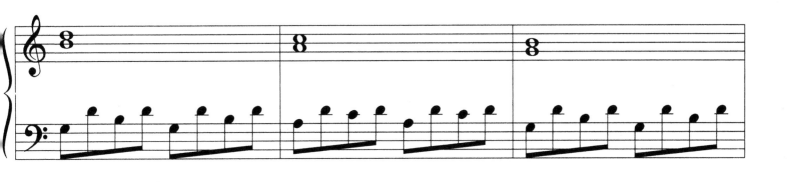

5. Goal Kick and Goal!

6. Finale